LET YOURSELF BE LOVED

LET YOURSELF BE
LOVED

TRANSFORMING FEAR INTO HOPE

PHILLIP BENNETT

Revised and Expanded Edition

Paulist Press
New York / Mahwah, NJ

Cover image by SergeyIT/Shutterstock.com
Cover design by Phyllis Campos
Book design by Lynn Else

Library of Congress Cataloging-in-Publication Data:

Bennett, Phillip, 1952-
    Let yourself be loved : transforming fear into hope / Phillip Bennett. — Revised and Expanded Edition.
        pages cm
    Includes bibliographical references.
    ISBN 978-0-8091-4918-6 (pbk. : alk. paper) — ISBN 978-1-58768-482-1
    1. God (Christianity)—Love. 2. Fear—Religious aspects—Christianity. 3. Spiritual life—Catholic Church. 4. Catholic Church—Doctrines. 5. Bennett, Phillip, 1952- I. Title.
    BT140.B46 2015
    231`.6—dc23
                                                                    2014033986

ISBN 978-0-8091-4918-6 (paperback)
ISBN 978-1-58768-482-1 (e-book)

Published by Paulist Press
997 Macarthur Boulevard
Mahwah, New Jersey 07430

www.paulistpress.com

Printed and bound in the
United States of America

For my parents May McKinney and Charles Bennett.
I miss you both dearly.

CONTENTS

FOREWORD

This little book can change your life, if you let it! The Rev. Dr. Phillip Bennett stands in a unique position to offer us wisdom for the *psyche*—which in Greek means both "mind" and "soul." His vocation has enabled him to speak from two worlds. As an Episcopal priest and spiritual director, he is well acquainted with the heights and depths of the spiritual journey, with its ups and downs, its times of feeling joyful closeness with God, and also the "dark nights of the soul" of which St. John of the Cross so eloquently and painfully wrote. As a psychologist and psychoanalyst, he is also well acquainted with the depths of our mental and emotional lives, and the ways in which the gifts and wounds of our personal history—especially in the vulnerable times of early childhood—have contributed to forming our personalities and our unique ways of viewing the world in which we live.

In this book, Bennett deftly blends spiritual wisdom with an appreciation for how we "tick" as persons, but it is much more than a secular self-help book. To quote Lauren Artress, a Canon priest at Grace Cathedral, San Francisco, who brought the spiritual practice of walking the labyrinth to North America—we are not just "human beings on a spiritual path," but we are (perhaps first and foremost) "spiritual beings on a human path." This book addresses the fullness of our lives as spiritual beings—body, mind, and spirit.

I have long kept the first edition of this book within easy reach. As a perfectionist myself, and someone whose critical nature has only been sharpened more and more in my professional life as both an artist and an academic, there was initially a part of me that looked at the book's title and gave a little silent sneer. "Yeah, right. Sounds like self-help poppycock!" Like many of us in both the Catholic and Protestant expressions of the Christian faith, I knew that Jesus said in the Gospel of John that he came that we might have life and have it abundantly (John 10:10), but my strict and proper New England upbringing did not convey that such abundance could come without a good measure of my own sweat, blood, and tears. If that sounds familiar, then try to get past the "curmudgeon" who lives inside each of us, full of criticism and warnings that we do not deserve God's love, and allow this book to become your friend. Give it a chance.

This book explores the many besetting fears that stand as obstacles in our way to knowing God and feeling God's love. Such fears come from inside ourselves, from the wounds life has handed us along the way, and from the influence of a society and world that values material wealth and power over spiritual wisdom and peace. But our fears are, in the end, a veil of illusion. If we allow ourselves to feel God's loving, knowing presence, we can get beyond them for a glimpse of the joy, the strength, and the peace that is truly what God desires for us and for all living beings. In this brief volume, Phillip Bennett brings both spiritual and psychological wisdom to the soul's deep question: Why don't we let ourselves fully know and feel God's love?

In one of the passages I have taken to heart, Bennett says that in his own life he struggled to know God's will as what God expected him to be and to do. But by following the suggestion of a Benedictine monk, he suspended his self-judgment and allowed himself simply to sit and be still in the presence of God. And he came to the realization that God's "will" was not a set of instructions to be followed to the letter (and hence subject to divine judgment), but "God's longing to draw me ever closer in intimate love and delight" (p. 3). This realization accords well with the literal meaning of the word for God's will in biblical Greek. *Will* is an English translation that conveys power and mastery and big demands—a mighty word befitting a sixteenth-century interpretation of a mighty ruling God. But the word may be better translated in our time not as God's "will" but as God's "desire." From the Greek word *theló*, meaning "to desire, want, or long for," God's *thelema* is God's desire for us and for all creation. God desires to be with us, and God desires our flourishing in joy and wellness.

This reframing of God's "will" is in the spirit of Bennett's book, where we also learn that God's judgment is not God's wish to punish us for wrongdoings, but God's deep knowledge of us, which sees and knows everything we are through the depth of God's love. "God's judgment," writes Bennett, "*is* God's love, in its penetrating, unremitting power....our layers of self-deception and avoidance of intimacy must be unwound until love can touch us to our core" (p. 22). As he concludes his chapter on the fear of judgment, "The judgment of love never injures our true self; it only releases it from constriction so that we may be the person we were created to be" (p. 23). In the words of the second-century theologian Saint Irenaeus, "The glory of God is the human person fully alive" (p. 51); this is what God desires for us. And as Bennett puts it, "Our worth does not lie in our productivity, our looks, or our 'usefulness.' We are the Beloved—that is our true, unshakeable identity" (p. 66).

This book is a modern spiritual classic. Keep it by your bedside or the place where you pray, reread the brief chapters and pray the poems and prayers included in each, as a reminder to "let yourself be loved!" Like me, you may also find yourself experiencing in the words of Saint Paul that "the peace of God, which surpasses all understanding, will guard your hearts and your minds in Christ Jesus" (Phil 4:7).

Let yourself be loved by this book!

The Rev. Pamela Cooper-White, PhD
Ben G. & Nancye Clapp Gautier
Professor of Pastoral Theology, Care and Counseling,
Columbia Theological Seminary, Decatur, Georgia

PREFACE

It has been nearly twenty years since this book was origi-
nally published. I wrote it because the theme resonated
deeply with me. It was something I needed to hear. I hoped
that it might be something some others needed to hear—
the good news that we are loved unconditionally as we are.
It seems to have resonated with many over the years for
which I am glad. I am grateful to be able to add further
thoughts that have come from further living. This newly
revised and expanded edition would not have come to be
without the strong encouragement and guidance of Paul
McMahon to whom I owe a tremendous debt of gratitude. I
am also grateful to Pamela Cooper-White for writing the
foreword. I am honored that she was willing to add her wise
voice. It is my hope that the book will continue to speak to
others who, like me, need to be reminded that it is in letting
ourselves be loved that we become bearers of love to others
and to this needy world.

INTRODUCTION

The Love That Casts Out Fear

There is no fear in love, but perfect love casts out fear;
for fear has to do with punishment, and whoever fears
has not yet reached perfection in love.
— 1 John 4:18

When I was twenty-two, I felt an urgency to decide my vocational future—an urgency not yet tempered by enough life experience to know that our most important life decisions often find us in unexpected ways. I wanted to know exactly what God's will for me was—now! While on retreat at a monastery, I met a monk named Benedict, whom I enlisted in my anxious search for God's will. He listened patiently as I spun out my concerns about finding the path God wanted me to take. When I had finished my stream of questions and confusions, he let a comfortable silence settle around us. Finally he responded, "As you describe your search for God's will, this image comes to me: God is like a recording full of instructions which you are trying to follow. However, the recording is playing in the next room with the door ajar and it is hard to make out all the words. You are trying to decipher what God is saying, but you are always a beat or two behind and so you can never be sure that you've got it exactly right."

The image jolted me. I had never thought of my quest to know God's will in this way. It seemed so inherently frustrating and uncertain. Then Benedict suggested an alternative image: "Imagine that God wants, more than anything, simply to be with you and delight in your presence. When you pray, instead of trying to listen to that recording in the next room, sit in a chair and imagine God in a chair right next to you. Just let yourself be in God's presence, without any agenda. Let God love you. See what happens."

Part of me found his suggestion wonderfully attractive, but another part of me thought it was too easy. Was God really this friendly and easygoing? Despite my misgivings, I took Benedict's advice and began "just sitting" in God's presence. In the silence, I tried to imagine God wanting to be with me, enjoying my presence. However, I soon discovered that I did not enjoy my own presence during these awkward sessions of silence. Without an agenda to focus on, all my mental demons began to rise up: restlessness, doubts, sadness, guilt, fear, anxiety, lack of self-love, anger, a need to control—they were all churning up as I struggled to imagine a loving God by my side.

After several days of "just sitting," very slowly, very subtly, I began to feel a Presence with me; a gentle, steady love that delighted in being with me. The Presence stirred delicately around the edge of my awareness, but would seem to recede if I tried to catch a direct glimpse of it. If I tried to clutch it, analyze it, make it do my bidding, it quickly vanished from my awareness. When I relaxed and gave up trying to make something happen, I again experienced the Presence holding me, sustaining me, loving me in wordless silence. It felt like a force both outside me and within me— a great, inexhaustible power, yet intimately near and gentle. I had begun praying in order to seek and find God, but instead I was discovering that God was seeking and finding me. I had set out to discover God's specific plan for my life—as if it were some divine blueprint. Instead, I was discovering another understanding of God's "will"—God's longing to draw me ever closer in intimate love and delight.

The wonderful news my friend Benedict brought me was that God truly delights in me—as I am. God enjoys being with me, as friends and lovers delight in being with each other. God wants me to be myself as I am; to relax, be real, and not to present myself in a certain way. The British pediatrician and psychoanalyst, D. W. Winnicott, speaks of a child's developing capacity to "be alone in the presence of another."[1] As children become more independent, they practice "being alone," absorbed in their own activity, but always with some reliable adult presence nearby. Periodically, children run back to mother or father to show the fruits of their activity. They are free to be themselves while knowing that a reliable adult is always nearby and available. For Winnicott, the "good-enough" parent neither impinges on the child's own space, nor abandons or ignores the child. Instead the child is allowed to simply *be* as him or herself. Winnicott's idea has rich implications for our relationship with God. Can we feel free simply to be ourselves in God's presence, trusting that God will allow us to relax and be ourselves without either impinging on us or abandoning us? When my own prayer began to shift from an anxious attempt to find out "what God wanted from me" to a growing trust that God simply wanted to *be* with me without any agenda, I was learning simply to "be alone in the presence of another." In not censoring my thoughts or trying to "please" God, I was discovering that I could be myself fully with a God who not only permitted but delighted in my freedom. This, says Winnicott, is what "good-enough" parents do; they allow children to play because they know they are safe. It is also what God does for us. Prayer—though often hard work—is also fundamentally an act of play, for it involves being ourselves in God's delighting presence.

An awareness of being loved unconditionally comes and goes. It is an experience of grace, which touches us from beyond our comprehension and control, often coming to us as an unbidden gift, breaking in on us with fresh power. When we feel the power of love, it is as if the veil of familiarity is lifted and we see more deeply into the mystery that is all around us. It may come to us in the beauty of a sunset, a strain of music, the ringing fullness of silence, sharing laughter with friends, a deep peace that descends on us in solitude, or watching someone we love as they sleep—at times like these, we get glimpses of the amazing preciousness of all life.

I have been privileged to hear many people share their spiritual journeys. Sometimes people are anxious that their experiences are not truly "religious" or "spiritual." They mistakenly believe that these experiences are reserved for religious "professionals" or those considered very advanced. However, in the spiritual life there are no experts, only beginners. When people realize that their religious experiences will not be judged, they begin to tell amazing stories of their spiritual journeys. I have always found these stories deeply moving. As I listen, I am convinced afresh of the power of God's love to touch us exactly at our point of need.

A woman I will call Margaret (all the names and other identifiers I use will be fictitious) told of an experience she had while cleaning her basement. "I was alone in the basement by myself cleaning. I felt heaviness in my heart, thinking about someone in my family who was seriously ill. I remember so clearly the exact moment when it happened—

I was sweeping the basement steps, watching the broom swinging back and forth. Suddenly, for no apparent reason, I looked up and I stood there—I don't know how long— with my eyes lighting on every detail in the basement: the sink with water dripping, the hum of the furnace, the piles of clothes and toys. Suddenly I realized I was not alone; there was a presence with me, a very tender presence that was drawing near to me, sharing my pain, and comforting me. Then, a great wave of love broke over me and I burst into tears of joy. As this love washed over me, I knew with deep certainty that this love had always been with me and would always be with me, no matter what happened to my loved ones or me. I also knew that this love extended to every person, every animal, every plant, every particle of the universe. I stood at the bottom of the basement steps with the broom in my hand, weeping for joy."

Unexpectedly, love had broken into Margaret's daily awareness. Although the emotional intensity and poignancy of the encounter has faded into the background of her awareness, it is now a powerful touchstone for her, always somewhere close to consciousness, reminding her that she is not alone, that she and everyone she meets is loved with the wonderful, all-embracing love that flooded her heart as she stood on her basement steps.

An experience of God's unconditional acceptance, such as Margaret's basement epiphany, takes time to integrate into everyday life. As the beauty of the experience fades, we often find it hard to sustain an awareness of God's loving presence —something in us pulls away; we become distracted, even resistant to an awareness of being loved. It is then that we need some regular spiritual practice to recollect us to God's presence. By placing ourselves intentionally in the presence of unconditional love—through prayer, meditation, reading, serving others—we return to the Mysterious Center beyond our ego's control and comprehension, which alone can calm our fears and ground us deeply in reality. In subtle ways, we find ourselves becoming more loving, less fearful and grasping. Slowly, like water wearing down a stone, the steady drops of love are washing away our fears. As we place ourselves daily under the stream of divine mercy, the living waters of love flow through us, slowly penetrating our fearful, dark recesses. The change that is wrought within us is gradual but deep; slow and subtle, but always profound.

It is now many years since my first awareness of the Presence as I sat in the silence. There are times when I am aware of God's love for me, and my life feels like a duet danced with the Divine Lover. However, often my awareness of love's presence fades and I act as if my life is a solo act. I still have resistance to simply letting myself be loved by God. I find many reasons to avoid the all-embracing Presence: I seek distractions, I turn my prayer into a project, I wander off in fantasies and planning. Like a fidgety child who climbs in and out of a parent's lap, I want God to hold me, but then I pull away. I do and I don't want to let myself be loved unconditionally. Such restlessness and ambivalence is a normal part of our human nature and nothing to be ashamed of. The important thing is simply to return again and again to the Font of our Being, and to draw from the waters of love. Letting ourselves be loved is the act of returning, again and again, to who we really are.

To the degree that we are unwilling to let go of our fixed view of ourselves and the world, we find the spaciousness of Unbounded Love threatening and unsettling. Our egos want to shrink things so that we still feel in control. However, letting ourselves be loved by God involves a radical receptivity. We can do nothing to earn love. We are naked, in need, and the recipients of free and unmerited love. It is easier to accept love if we believe we have "earned" it. In this way, we can still receive love on our own terms, keeping ourselves at the center of our world. We cling to our role as giver and so avoid confronting what Christian theologian Johannes Metz calls "poverty of spirit";[2] the awareness that we cannot meet our own deepest desires through our own power.

As we become increasingly aware of God's love for us, we begin to see others, and all creation, through the eyes of love. Our fearful and constricted hearts begin to open to the joyful awareness that there is more than enough love to go around. No one is more deserving of love than another. Although this is ultimately a joyful change, it also stretches us, calling us to move beyond our self-absorption, to break out of our familiar ruts, and to sojourn into the spaciousness of a new and unfamiliar land.

Despite all our continued resistance, unconditional love is always there waiting for us. When we have run through our many ways of resisting, love is there with arms outstretched, waiting to embrace us as we are. When we complicate our lives by imagining problems that never come to pass, love is there to untangle the gnarled web of our anxieties. When we play our mental movies of imagined glory—or failure—love is there as the solid Ground right beneath our feet, inviting us to take the next step back into reality. When we discover in our hearts a mysterious sadness, an unexpected anger, a vague, unnamable fear, love is there with us—not to take away the feeling, but to meet us in it. As we open daily to the love that surrounds us, we become increasingly sure that we can trust this love to be there, no matter what life may bring.

The lessons of love take a lifetime of learning. No one is a graduate, for there is no final point of arrival. No one

ever moves completely beyond the ambivalence and ambi-
guity of our human experience into some anxiety-free state
of certainty. The process of learning to be loved and to love
is messy, unpredictable, spontaneous, and surprising. There
is no perfect way to do it; all that matters is to keep loving
and allowing ourselves to be loved. Our attempts at chisel-
ing away our own anxieties and distractions never succeed,
but we are promised that "perfect love casts out fear" (1 John
4:18). This casting out continues over our lifetime.

We will never outgrow our fears completely; they will
return again and again. This is normal because they are a
part of our natural human frailty. Instead of trying to control our fears, we need to pray out of the depths of them, to
embrace our poverty of spirit, our continual need for
strength and reassurance. When we try to quell our fears
through our own defensive maneuvers—through denial,
worrying, overcompensation, distraction, trying to earn
approval—we only give them more power. However, when
we realize that our need for love is at the root of all fears, we
can open ourselves to the inflowing of love, letting ourselves
be loved as we are, not as we would wish to be. This can lead
to a deeper acceptance of self and others. We can return to
the amazing truth that God longs to give us "abundantly far
more than all we can ask or imagine" (Ephesians 3:20).

Let us now look at some of the fears that keep us from
letting ourselves be loved. These fears I discuss are not an
exhaustive list, nor are they neatly separable into distinct
categories. Usually, we find them jumbled together in a con-
fusing welter. Our fears often arise in our psychological
blind spots, making it difficult to recognize their power and
persistence. If we try to run from them or eradicate them, we
only give them more power. As we grow more conscious of
our besetting fears, the key is not to judge them nor try too

hard to get rid of them. Instead, we need to extend to the fearful parts of ourselves the same kind of compassion and patience we would extend to someone we love. Only by befriending the fears in our hearts do we give up trying to control them and simply open our hearts so that love may work its deep healing within us.

CHAPTER 1

FEAR OF OPENING OLD WOUNDS

We must come to love our wounds.
— Friedrich Nietzsche

Lucia, a woman in my former parish, was diagnosed with liver cancer in her mid-fifties. She was an intensely private person, with a thick emotional shell that kept others from getting too close. She was respected for her efficiency at work and in her volunteer duties at the church but she had little social life. When not at work or at church, she retreated to her small efficiency apartment where she lived as a recluse.

Then cancer struck. Little by little she began to risk reaching out to a few people in the parish. As she let them know of her cancer, people offered their support, but as soon as she opened the door to let someone into her life, she slammed it shut in the person's face. Lucia was fortunate to be surrounded by people who were ready to love her for the long haul, even when she tried to reject their love and return to her isolation.

Love pierces to the core of who we are. And when love touches us to the core, it also touches the pain we carry inside us. What I did not know until her last days was that Lucia had suffered a great wounding from love. As a young woman, she had been engaged to a Protestant seminarian who suddenly broke off the engagement with little explanation. Lucia was sent reeling, and in her hurt and anger she pulled inside herself and shut the door. Like Charles Dickens's Miss Havisham in *Great Expectations*, she had locked her heart away where no one could touch it, mourning for a groom who would never come.

As the cancer worsened, Lucia had to quit her job, being stripped of her last bastion of self-definition. She was no longer valued for her efficiency and helpfulness; now she was the one being helped. After several hospital stays, members of the parish convinced her to come home and let them provide round-the-clock hospice care. Her already slender body became increasingly frail, and her skin and eyes grew more jaundiced each day. Although she seemed less resistant to being cared for, she still kept her suit of armor in place even as her privacy and health were being stripped away.

The summer came and Lucia continued her slow decline. I had just returned from vacation, not having seen her for several weeks. She was now almost a skeleton. However, it was not her withered body that caught my eye as I walked into her room—it was her *eyes*. They were fully alive, completely open channels through which I could see right into her, and she was looking directly into me. There were no longer any walls; no more shame or fear. I was so stunned that the first thing I said was, "Lucia, what's happened to you?" A broad, radiant smile broke across her face. She replied, "I finally let God love me! I really know God loves me and that other people love me!" I could see the love welling up in her eyes. She was a transformed person, radiant, on fire, even as her body was passing away.

Lucia's funeral was like no other I remember, for everyone who had gathered around her had seen the fire in her eyes and knew it was love that had worked this amazing transformation. In her face, we had seen the glory of God shining, showing us a foretaste of what was in store for all of us. The image of her radiant eyes continues to point the way for me, reminding me that when I let down my walls, love can work miracles of transformation.

Whether we resist until our death like Lucia, or open up earlier in life, the challenge is the same for all of us: to choose the pain of opening up old wounds over the pain of sealing them off. Either way, we will experience pain. We will, as T. S. Eliot said, be "consumed by either fire or fire."[1] The fire of fear makes our life a living hell of isolation and unshared pain, but the fire of love cauterizes, heals, and frees us.

Going into our pain can be frightening. The intensity of the hurt may feel as if it will overwhelm us. However, if we close our hearts in order to avoid further hurt, we also close ourselves to the transforming power of love. We may need to find a trusted friend or a trained professional who can accompany us on our healing journey. When our moods become too intense or unstable, we should also consider medical help, because medication may help us considerably if there is a biological component to our suffering. Support and recovery groups can also provide safe places where we can share our stories of suffering and grace, discovering that our pain can become a bridge connecting us with others.

Pain, when embraced instead of denied, can become a precious gift that deepens our compassion for others. In novelist Frederick Buechner's words, we are called to be good "stewards of our pain,"[2] not burying our pain but investing it. In a mysterious way, sharing our pain, instead of hiding it, can bring healing not only to ourselves but to those around us. Within the hidden pain often lie the seeds of new growth.

The place where we are hurt is also the place where we can come to know love in new and surprising ways.

As we do battle with our demons and come out the other side, we become bearers of hope to others; our authority comes from our genuine encounter with our psychic depths. We, like Jacob, have wrestled with our dark angel and have received both a wound and a blessing. In some paradoxical way, the wound actually becomes the blessing. No wonder, then, that the verb *to wound* in French is *blesser*. When we have gone into the pain, instead of running from it, we discover new hope and compassion that has been forged in the fire of suffering. To the degree that we have embraced our pain, we, like Jesus, have descended into hell, have gone all the way down into our own darkness and despair and have come out the other side into the resurrection life.

The words *wound* and *wonder* share a common root which means "to penetrate." Our wounds are the places where life has penetrated us. These places can become infected and closed off or they can become channels that open us to fuller life and love. As we experience the healing power of love, we do not merely survive our wounds: we are shaped by them and find new energy in them. Many of us in helping professions would never have developed our sensitivity to others' pain if we had not suffered ourselves. Truly effective helpers are those who have walked the same road as those they are helping. As Henri Nouwen reminds us, genuine healers are always wounded healers who find in their own wounds reservoirs of compassion and wisdom from which they can draw when ministering to others.[3]

As we experience healing, our wounds never really go away; instead, as they heal, they become deep wells within us in which we may feel the pain of the world and respond, not with the hollow optimism of those who run from their suffering, but as those who have learned to trust a healing power at work even in the bleakest hours of life. The Risen Christ never loses his wounds, even in his resurrection body. His wounded hands, feet, and side identify him to his loved ones; they are the unmistakable signs that he has been through death and has returned victorious. So too with us, our wounds become signs of hope to others that it is possible to die and rise again; to come out the other side of suffering and despair.

PRAYER

O God,
for so long I hid my wounds
both from myself and others,
feeling ashamed, isolated,
secretly hopeless
that they could be healed.
Now I can see how deeply
my wounds unite me to every person
and to all of life.
We all suffer,
we are all wounded by life.
Thank you that my wounds
become channels of your grace
if I but trust your healing power.
Thank you that my wounds identify me—
just as the Risen Christ is known
by his glorious scars.
Although I once could not
have imagined it,
my wounds have become

something wonderful—
a bridge to life
instead of a barrier;
an inexhaustible
well of life
instead of a bottomless
abyss of despair.
Through my wounds
your love has penetrated
me to my core
and in them I have
mined the jewels of your grace.
For this unspeakable gift
I thank you with
an overflowing heart.

CHAPTER 2

FEAR OF JUDGMENT

My highest ambition is to be who I already am.
—Thomas Merton

The fear of judgment is a universal human condition. Even the most self-confident of us harbor secret doubts about ourselves—doubts about our worth, our accomplishments, our acceptability. These doubts are amazingly persistent, despite our attempts to reassure ourselves with "rational" estimations of our worth. Our fear of judgment arises out of *shame*—that incredibly painful state in which we feel there is something defective and embarrassing about who we are. Guilt is about what we *do* but shame is about who we *are*. When we are ashamed, we do not want to be seen; we want to hide from the judging eyes we think others will cast on us.

A man near forty whom I will call David is always impeccably dressed for his therapy sessions. He is quite successful as an architect and is highly regarded in his field. Yet, when he first came to see me for psychotherapy, David was tortured by self-judgment. He felt he was a boring, hollow person, trying unsuccessfully to con the world into believing he was interesting. His frequent refrain was, "If people could see into me and know how little there is inside, they would never want to spend time with me." He spoke of his "demon" of self-judgment, who sat on his shoulder whispering harsh, despairing messages. Our work was long and slow, helping him to realize that his "critical demon" need not have the final word. One evening, he went to a party and was surprised and delighted to enjoy himself without his demon ruining everything. He was animated as he described this new experience: "I had this glimpse of really liking myself, of knowing I'm a worthwhile person. It came and went, but at least I felt it briefly." Predictably, it wasn't long before his demon of self-judgment came swooping down again: "Whom are you trying to kid? You can't sustain this kind of spontaneity; you'll always be this way; stop trying to fight it." This self-judging voice was still fierce, but now there was another competing voice that David dubbed his Good Demon. He imagined his warring demons sitting on either shoulder, whispering their conflicting messages in his ear. As David felt increasingly more alive and less self-judging, his Bad Demon shrank and his Good Demon grew stronger.

One day, David shared a memory of golf balls, which he and his brother collected when they were boys. They lived next to a golf course and spent free time combing the area for stray balls. David had always imagined that the golf balls were hollow at their core. Finally, he and his brother broke one open, unwinding the rubber bands inside: "It seemed like there were miles of this rubber band–like material. I was sure we would find a hollow center when we unwound this mass of rubber string. However, I was surprised to find this very small but dense core at the center. I see that golf ball as a metaphor for myself: I used to be afraid to unwrap all the layers inside me for fear that I would find an empty core. But instead I've found myself, and it's solid. It's such a relief. I want to tell other people who feel hollow and worthless that they really are worthwhile. Thank God I've finally been able to experience this solid part of myself."

David had touched a core in himself that was not of his own making and therefore beyond his judgment. Despite his shameful feelings of being defective, he was discovering that he was loveable, not for what he did, but for who he *was*. He was lovable because he was made in the image of love. As the battle between the two demons increased, David began to talk explicitly about spiritual concerns, describing how he had prayed to find a way through his fear and lack of self-confidence: "Recently I did something I haven't done since I was a child: I got down on my knees and prayed to God, saying, 'I want to feel fully alive. I want to feel it all—the joy and the pain.'"

David was discovering his self-worth not only as other people mirrored it back to him, but as Being itself mirrored it to him. Only this affirmation from Ultimate Being could free him from his crippling dependence on validation from others or himself. David's experience of a solid inner core resonates with many of the great spiritual teachers who image God residing at the center of the human soul. Only by returning continually to this unshakable center of Being within us, can we find freedom from our withering self-judgment and the shame that drives it.

Why do we feel these self-judgments even when the more rational part of ourselves knows we are all right as we are? In his "Self Psychology," psychoanalyst Heinz Kohut, describes how we develop our sense of self through our early interactions with others.[1] As children, others mirror back to us our existence and worth. People hold us, talk to us, play with us, praise us, and so let us know we are important and lovable. In time, children internalize the mirroring they receive from others, carrying their own inner sense of worth. Our self-esteem comes from being esteemed by others and taking that esteem into ourselves. However, our need for mirroring and validation does not end with childhood. Even the most self-confident person needs continual validation throughout life; we can never get enough affirmation. Because our need for validation is endless, we face a dilemma when we continue to seek it only from other people or from possessions or accomplishments, for all these sources can give us only a partial and transitory affirmation. In time—if we are honest with ourselves—we discover, with Augustine of Hippo, that our hearts are, indeed, restless until they find their rest in God. God alone has an unlimited capacity to mirror our own worth to us and give us the continual affirmation we need, even to our dying breath. This does not mean that affirmation from other people is not important or that it can be sidestepped by going to God. That would be to misuse our spiritual practice as a way of avoiding the messy and transforming experience of human love. However, we must also come to realize that other people are not God; they can only give us partial affirmation.

Just as we must not look to others for our ultimate identity, so we must not look even to ourselves. In order to let ourselves be loved unconditionally by God, we must confront our strong attachment to our self-images. The contemplative psychiatrist Gerald May, reminds us that "attachment" comes from the old French "nailed to": when we take our self-images as the final word about ourselves, we feel we have ourselves nailed down, defined, and understood.[2] We think we really *are* these images and either cling to the positive ones (attachment) or run from the negative ones (aversion). However, to the degree that we run toward or away from these self-images, we lose our freedom simply to *be*, without judgments or conditions. Both running toward and running away from these images limit our inner freedom and alienate us from Being. Although "positive" self-images may seem more helpful, they bring only temporary relief from our insecurity and self-doubt, because living up to our own positive self-images can be as exhausting and enslaving as our negative self-images. In fact, these positive self-images can set us up for self-judgment: when we do not live up to our own expectations, we find ourselves suddenly deflated, depressed, and self-judging. In Kohut's terms, we oscillate between a "grandiose" self-image, which is too big, too good, too shaky, and the "narcissistic injury" that comes when that grandiose image is punctured. For example, we may pride ourselves on being loving and sensitive, strongly needing others to see us this way, but when we are criticized for being uncaring, it feels devastating, as if our whole identity is being challenged and undermined.

As we cling to our self-images, we are bound in a continual cycle of inflation and deflation, unable to rest simply in being ourselves without categories and judgments. The liberating truth we need to hear is that our worth and identity have nothing to do with our positive or negative self-representations. They are *not* our true identity, no matter how real and substantial they may seem to us. Our true identity can only be found in our Loving Creator, who has created us for an intimate relationship. Only as we return to the One who is at the core of our being can we find release from the self-images that we cling to or run from. There is a great paradox here: we must empty ourselves of our carefully constructed "selves" in order to be filled with the fullness of our true self. We must release our fierce grip on our self-created identity in order to discover our identity in Being. As we loosen our attachment to our self-images, we are met by God who is already within us, waiting to embrace and affirm us as we are. We discover that we are *already* validated, simply for being ourselves, for being alive.

Given the destructive nature of our self-judgment, what are we to make of all the images of *God's* judgment in our religious Scriptures and Traditions? How can we reconcile God's love with God's judgment? The most satisfying answer I have found is that God's judgment *is* God's love, in its penetrating, unremitting power. God's judgment is never divorced from God's love; it is not some angry part of God, which is split off from God's mercy and gentleness. Instead, God's judgment is the way we experience pure and constant love that sees and knows us to our core. Being known so deeply is like David's golf ball: our layers of self-deception and avoidance of intimacy must be unwound until love can touch us to our core.

Sometimes we fear that God's judgment will hurt us. We have difficulty imagining that God will not inflict the same hurt and shame on us that we have inflicted on ourselves or have suffered at the hands of others. In C. S. Lewis's *The Voyage of the Dawn Treader*,[3] the sour and willful boy, Eustace, strays off by himself and finds a cave full of golden jewelry. Unbeknownst to him, the cave and jewelry belong to a dragon he has just seen die. Eustace greedily grabs the most beautiful piece of jewelry, a large golden bracelet, and slides it on his arm. He then drifts off to sleep beside a fire in the dragon's cave. He awakens to an excruciating pain in his upper arm, for where there had been human flesh, Eustace now has dragon flesh and the bracelet is cutting into his swollen, scaly body. Finally, he meets up with Aslan the lion, who assures him he can pierce Eustace's dragon body with his claws, just far enough to cut through the dragon flesh without hurting the little boy within. This is a great test for Eustace and for each of us: trusting that the penetrating judgment of God's love will cut just far enough to remove all the tough scales we have grown around us to protect us from pain, without damaging our true selves that lie beneath.

God's judgment is the penetrating aspect of God's love, purging, purifying, and stripping away tough old skin. The judgment of love never injures our true self; it only releases it from constriction so that we may be the person we were created to be.

PRAYER

My God,
a voice within me sometimes
judges me harshly.
I lose touch with that
solid core of goodness within me
which comes from you.
When I am seduced by
images of myself that
inflate or deflate,
help me return to you,
the core of my being.
Be my mirror
in which I may
behold myself undistorted,
seen through
the eyes of your love.
Help me know that
your judgment is always
the other side of your love;
the purging fire of your

infinite compassion
drawing me
and all creation
to yourself.

CHAPTER 3

FEAR OF INTIMACY

True union does not confound but differentiates.
—Pierre Teilhard de Chardin

Love is never abstract. It is only real as we live it out in the daily give and take of our lives. We never become ourselves in isolation, for we are made in the Likeness of a God who is relationship—this is what we mean when we speak of the Trinity—it is a way of saying that relationship is at the very heart of creation. The universe is a great relationship of the one and the many knit together. This is becoming increasingly clearer as science reveals the amazingly intricate web that connects subatomic quarks with the farthest galaxies. We can speak in lofty platitudes about love, but when we live "up close and personal," we are stretched and challenged. In our close relationships, it is hard to keep up pretense; we know and we are known. Sometimes this feels good; sometimes it is unsettling. In intimacy we can no longer hide; we are seen not as we wish to appear, but as we really are. This nakedness can ultimately be liberating, but like all self-knowledge, it can be unsettling and uncomfortable.

Intimacy is like a crucible in which the gold of love is being refined: things can heat up and become volatile; they may grow tepid and boring; they may grow icy and frozen.

Whatever the temperature and chemistry in love's crucible, it is only through commitment over time that the deep transformation of intimacy occurs. When I prepare couples for marriage I often say, "You are going to learn more about yourselves and your partner than you could ever imagine. Sometimes this will feel like good news and sometimes like bad news. However, if you stick with it, even in the hard times, you will come to know yourself and the other more and more deeply." This is what Pema Chodron calls "the wisdom of no escape."[1] When we block the exits, we have to stay and learn instead of running away.

Intimacy requires navigation between two anxieties: the fear of losing ourselves or losing the other person. Challenging questions may arise: Must we sacrifice parts of ourselves in order to stay connected? Will we lose our closeness if we experience significant differences? These are questions with which a young couple wrestles as they sit in my office. They describe their clashes over wiping off the kitchen sink—he insists on this as if it is some necessary cosmic order. She chafes at his demand and wipes the sink a few times, then neglects it in her passive-aggressive rebellion. Of course, their conflict is about everything *but* the kitchen sink! It is about whether they still have individual autonomy even though they are now a couple sharing the same space. Is there still room for a genuinely separate "Me" and "You" in their "We"? Can they learn to compromise without feeling that they have capitulated? Can they tolerate, let alone celebrate, each other's significant differences? These are challenges they may have to revisit over and over through the years, because relationships evolve as people change through the seasons of their lives.

When we fear merger or abandonment—whether with another person or with God—we still imagine that we must make a choice to be either separate or connected. In truth, this is always a false choice, for genuine love draws us into union where we can become more fully ourselves, delighting in each other's individuality. Our connectedness depends on our separateness and our separateness depends on our connectedness. However, this is often not the message that has been communicated about love. Family systems therapist Murray Bowen speaks of "enmeshment"—an emotional stuck-togetherness, in which family members assume that they must all think and feel the same way.[2] Individual differences are seen as threatening to the family unity. In this atmosphere of oppressive conformity, all disagreements must either be covered over with a false compliance, or a family member must make an "emotional cutoff," trying to put emotional and often physical distance between themselves and the family. But, says Bowen, the farther we run from our families, the more we are controlled by their emotional force field. Only by learning to speak our own truth nonreactively in love do we become more honest with our families while at the same time coming to accept (though not always to like) them as they are.

Martin Buber speaks of two different ways we can relate to people. One is the "I/It" mode.[3] In this stance, others exist as extensions of our own reality, our own needs, and our own agendas. The other way of relating is "I/Thou" in which we see the sacredness of others in their own right. They are an amazing universe of their own, existing apart from our projections and agendas—unique expressions of the Sacred Ground from which we all come and to which we will all return. I remember my first time truly experiencing the power and mystery of the "I/Thou" way of seeing. A high school friend was in great pain because of his father's alcoholism and his parents' impending divorce. He felt like an orphan, like no one really knew him or loved him for who he was. As he was telling his story, suddenly I felt as if I was lifted out of the ordinariness of the moment, like some movie in which things go in slow motion and the sound track goes quiet. I watched his lips move but wasn't listening to his words. Instead, I simply stared at him realizing that he was a whole other living, breathing mystery. When we see the world in this "I/Thou" way—even for a moment—everyone, whether stranger, friend, or lover, becomes for us a living, breathing icon of the Divine.

Realizing that we are loved unconditionally by God can help us get beyond our defensive self-protection and see the infinite preciousness of every person, every creature, on this amazing planet. The veil of familiarity is stripped away and, at least for a fleeting moment, we can say of every person we meet what Jacob said as he was reunited with his estranged brother, Esau: "Truly to see your face is like seeing the face of God" (Genesis 33:10). This capacity to see into the heart of things as God sees is a precious gift of the Spirit, which calls us beyond our narrow, self-protective shell.

Intimacy opens up the inevitability of loss. The more we love, the greater the pain when we are separated. The adage "It is better to have loved and lost than never to have loved at all" is hardly a comfort when we are in the throes of deep grief. What we want is to love and never to lose, but in this life loss is inevitable. Opening our heart means that it will surely be broken; grief is the price we will pay for love. Loss is inevitable but the way we respond to it is not. When our hearts are broken, we may become bitter and rigid, unwilling to risk loving again. Or, we may choose—and what a hard choice it is!—to let our hearts be broken open, but deciding not to close our hearts to love. Our willingness to be broken open presumes some basic trust in life, for in

order to let go, we have to believe that something or someone will catch us as we fall. To the degree that we have not
felt secure in our past relationships, it is very hard to give
ourselves fully in intimacy for fear that the pain of loss will
eclipse the joy of loving.

In his writings on parent-child attachment, the English
psychiatrist John Bowlby speaks of the importance of having a "secure base" from which to move into the world with
confidence.[4] If a child experiences early love and reliability
from parents, a "secure attachment" develops that allows
the child to face unknown or fearful situations with an
awareness of being loved and protected. However, without
this secure attachment, the child is prone to separation anxiety, or may be unable to form any deep attachments at all.
Although our early relationships strongly shape us, Bowlby
believes that, as adults, we may still be able to make up for
the secure base we didn't get early in life by finding people
who can provide the nurturing and reliability we need.
Bowlby's ideas, though useful, have a limit, because in this
life there is no absolutely secure base. We will be separated,
sooner or later, from those we love.

In letting ourselves be loved by God, we form an attachment to the only One who cannot leave us. Even our most
intimate human relationships cannot fulfill all our needs; to
expect this is a kind of idolatry in which we put others in the
place of God. Our relationships are meant to circle around
a greater Center to whom we must all turn for unconditional
love. When we are in touch with this Center, we are free to
love each other deeply without possessiveness, realizing we
have been given to each other as fellow travelers as we share
this journey on earth. In the crucible of intimacy, we grow
into greater wholeness both individually and together. We
go through many seasons together and separately. We never

graduate from the School of Love—there are endless lessons to learn. Through it all, we are being refined by the fires of grace so that the life of the Beloved may be made flesh in us more and more.

PRAYER

My God,
in your Triune life
there is room for all.
You create us to be separate yet deeply connected.
When my anxiety moves me toward merger or flight,
help me to remember that true union
joins without melding;
true autonomy is rooted in interdependence.
Teach me that deep fidelity to myself
is also fidelity to others and to you.
O Spacious Intimacy,
teach me to love
so that I am neither too close
nor too far from others.
Draw me deeper into this Dance of Love
where our distances touch
and our intimacy leaves
sacred space for all.

CHAPTER 4

FEAR OF ANGER

Anybody can become angry—that is easy, but to be angry with the right person for the right purpose, and in the right way—that is not easy.

—Aristotle

We are perhaps the most vulnerable when we are angry. We lose our composure; our hearts race, our faces flush. Even when we try to hide our anger, our voices often give us away. Anger, in itself, is not something to be ashamed of. It is rooted in our self-protective animal instincts. When we perceive a threat, our bodies are finely attuned to protect us by a sudden rush of adrenaline that propels us either to fight or flee. Although anger may serve us well as a primary survival mechanism, it can often be more a liability than an aid in our everyday lives. It exposes the rawest layers of our creaturely nature and often leaves us more vulnerable than protected. After the first wave of anger, there is often a second wave of shame.

Sometimes we have received the message—whether overt or covert—that love and anger are incompatible. This creates an impossible dilemma: if we love we cannot be angry, and if we are angry we cannot love. On a rational level, we may have no problem with the idea of love and anger coexisting, but because anger has the potential to cause injury, it can be hard to accept it as a normal part of relationships—especially intimate ones. Religious people, in particular, often have trouble with anger, thinking it is "unspiritual." This misunderstanding can cause repression of angry feelings. However, although anger is consciously denied, we can smell it in the air! I had a college friend who had the annoying habit of always opening the door for others and refusing to let anyone open it for him. He was bent on a kind of false humility that thinks love is only about giving and not receiving. One day I had grown so tired of his controlling courtesy that I refused to let him open the door for me. I opened the door and waited for him, but he stood there refusing to enter. He became furious! Beneath his generosity was a strong layer of anger and control.

Our anxiety over being angry can be transferred to God: If I let myself feel angry at God, will God still love me? Will I be accepted as I am—including my anger? Do I have to be "justified" in my anger or can I simply let myself be vulnerable, trusting that God desires intimacy with me in *all* parts of myself—including my anger? The writer of the Psalms provides a colorful example of being angry at God. He rants and rails against God when he is feeling neglected, mistreated, or abandoned:

> Rouse yourself! Why do you sleep, O Lord?
>   Awake, do not cast us off forever!
> Why do you hide your face?
>   Why do you forget our affliction and oppression?
>   (Psalm 44:23–24)

The psalmist shares the full range of his feelings with God—from joy, gratitude, and praise, to anger, bitterness, and despair. It is all part of his intimate conversation with God. He does not try to tidy himself up. Theresa of Avila literally could not tidy herself up when, during a miserable trip to deal with obstinate, uncooperative fellow nuns and all sorts of other misfortunes, she was thrown by a stubborn donkey into a muddy stream. She was reported to have shaken her fist at God and shouted, "If this is the way you treat your friends, no wonder you have so few of them!"

While it is true that anger has the potential to form a wall, it can sometimes be a bridge. It can serve a healthy function when it shows us that something important needs to be addressed so that distance and resentment do not grow. This healthy anger can be a form of *communication* in which we step out and take the risk to speak the truth in love. The courage to be honest always carries the risk of rejection, but the risk is worth taking, if it can strengthen communication and trust.

Contemporary studies of childhood development show that it is not the lack of ordinary conflict that helps a child develop strong, healthy relationships. Rather, it is the repeated experience of *rupture and repair*. Exercise can cause small tears in a muscle which, when healed, make the muscle larger and stronger. Similarly, love grows stronger and more resilient as we experience forgiveness and reconciliation over and over. There are inevitable times of injury, but these can be opportunities to strengthen the bond of love. Madeline L'Engle describes her own experience of this in her marriage:

> There have been times when I've been so angry or so hurt that I thought my love would never recover. And then, in the midst of near despair...I am returned to a state of love again—till next time....I can say no more than that this is mystery, and gift, and that somehow or other, through grace, our failures can be redeemed and blessed.[1]

Some anger may be righteous. It can be a proper indignation at injustice and mistreatment of others that calls us to take action in order to address wrongs and to work for good. In our personal lives, this righteous anger may call us to wrestle with hard choices, such as whether to stay in or leave abusive relationships and groups. Whatever the context, it is important to discern the difference between righteous anger and *self*-righteous anger. This is not always easy to do or to do quickly—especially when we are feeling reactive.

Sometimes anger is passed down through the generations. When old family wounds are transferred, we may find ourselves reenacting the hurtful patterns of relating that we grew up with and vowed never to repeat. My father had intense mood swings: he could be sweet and loving at one moment and then enraged at the next. I loved my father deeply and knew, even as a child, that his anger came from a split-off part of himself that was deeply wounded. I tried not to let his anger upset me too much, knowing that he was "not himself" in his dark moods and that his angry storms would pass. I took the role of the calm and rational one, but of course anger was building up inside me. I vowed never to repeat this pattern of unjust anger, but later as an adult I was appalled to hear some of the same anger coming out of my mouth! When we are in the grip of transgenerational anger, old family ghosts come alive in us. These psychic ghosts can get particularly activated in our close relationships.

Sometimes we turn our anger on ourselves. This may feel safer, because we avoid conflict and possible rejection from others, but it takes a tremendous toll on our self-esteem and makes it hard to trust that we will be loved and accepted as we are. We become impatient and unforgiving toward ourselves in a way that would strike us as sad and unjust, if we saw someone else doing it to themselves. A helpful exercise in dealing with self-anger is to ask what we would say to another person who was in our position. Almost invariably people say things like, "I would tell that person not to be so hard on herself," or "I would tell him to be more patient and forgiving towards himself." We can often speak a word of consolation to others that we find difficult to speak to ourselves.

Of course, there is unhealthy anger. It can become toxic and mesmerizing. In the theatre of our mind, we keep replaying the insults and injustices done to us. There can be a certain perverse enjoyment in savoring our anger. Like a dog gnawing a bone, we chew on it with a single-minded intensity, sucking its bitter but intoxicating flavor. The desert fathers and mothers of the third century AC were careful observers of the passions of the human heart. They believed that troubling states of mind were not in themselves unhealthy or sinful. Following the admonishment of Ephesians 4:26 (be angry but don't let your anger control you), they accepted anger as a natural emotion, but one that could become unhealthy if it turned to what they called "wrath." The Greek word is *orge*—which means "to teem" or "to swell," and can be used to describe ripening fruit. This is not a sudden outburst of anger, but the slowly, carefully nursed anger that grows and swells like some dark fruit of the heart. We lose our calmness of mind and we cannot pray. We do not want to release our grip on this kind of toxic anger, because it feeds the seductive illusion of our *false innocence*. In fact, the temptation to false innocence is especially powerful when we have been wronged. There are times to be rightly angry and not to offer cheap and premature forgiveness, but if we focus only on what others have done to us, we become blind to our capacity to transgress against others. We build up a wall of self-righteousness and hide behind it in self-defense. Whether our wrath is a raging fire or a hidden icy stream that runs silently below the surface, it cuts us off from feeling our common humanity with those who anger and hurt us. The desert fathers and mothers taught that the antidote to this destructive anger is love and humility. When we love we become grounded again, we return to our right minds; we dethrone ourselves from the judgment seat. We stop trying to play God.

Anger calls us to discernment: if we simply try to push it down, we give it more power. However, if we simply indulge it, we lose a chance for deeper self-examination. When we can make a space for our anger in prayerful contemplation and reflection, we may begin to discern its deeper roots. In this way, anger can be a spiritual friend and teacher in disguise. If we can approach our anger with interest and compassion, it can be a mirror that shows us the state of our soul at any moment. Instead of trying to justify, suppress, or get rid of our anger, we can approach it with compassionate curiosity: What is at the heart of my anger? What can it tell me about the present state of my heart? What am I feeling beneath my anger? Hurt? Fear? Insecurity? Powerlessness? Grief? Despair? This approach is also important in relating to others' anger. When we can listen beneath their words and actions for their emotional pain and insecurity, we can begin to see them with the new eyes of compassion. Our anger softens and we realize that we are all in the same boat of humanity.

Allowing ourselves to be loved by God means we are accepted with our anger, not in spite of it. This most vulnerable and sometimes volatile part of ourselves is a vital part of our humanity, and so God accepts it and seeks to be with us in it. Sometimes our anger may feel like a barrier to love, but God's love is bigger than our anger and the shame that often comes when we feel it. God's love is able to penetrate our anger and speak peace to our hearts. In the midst of or after the storm of anger, God's calming voice is speaking, "I accept you as you; I accept your anger and the feelings that lie beneath it. You do not have to hide. I can take your anger, absorb it, and purify it. Your anger cannot defeat my love."

PRAYER

My God,
I feel anger rising within me;
it is bubbling up;
I am on the edge of losing control.
I feel hurt, mistreated,
and I want to strike back.
Help me to discern what to do with this anger.
Is it calling me to communicate,
to risk speaking an uncomfortable truth in love?
Is it calling me to look into my own heart?
to see what fears and vulnerabilities lie beneath?
Calm and center me now
so that I am not blinded by anger.
Help me breathe and think.
O Merciful One
your love is bigger than all my anger.
Help me to return to you My Center.
Steady me until this storm has passed.

CHAPTER 5

FEAR OF LOSS

I am lavish with riches made from loss.
—May Sarton

In this life there is no escape from loss. Everything passes, nothing stays the same. "For here we have no lasting city, but we are looking for the city that is to come" (Hebrews 13:14). We try to deny the fundamental impermanence of things because loss will bring us pain. There are many deaths we must face in this life. Physical death is the biggest of them, but there are others, small or great, sudden or slow. We may suffer the loss of health, mental functioning, job, and professional identity. We may lose our home or have to move from familiar surroundings. Institutions may die, churches may close, neighborhoods may change, whole cultures may come to an end. Furthermore, there is the advancing loss that looms over our planet: our destruction of the earth's natural balance that is causing seas to rise, whole species to die out, and people—especially the poor—to suffer more and more.

Not all losses are ultimately bad; some may be part of necessary and creative change. It may be time to move on, time to let go of the old and make room for the new. Yet, even when loss may be necessary and life-giving, there is often grief. There is no way to short-circuit our grief, for it has its own life and rhythm; it comes in waves that only gradually lessen in intensity, sometimes flooding over us again when we least expect it. It cannot be rushed, even when those around us may wish it were shortened to ease their own discomfort. A woman who had lost her husband put it this way, "When he first died, everyone was so supportive. However, after a few months, most people stoppped asking me how I was doing. Maybe they thought that they would upset me, or cause my grief to be prolonged—I don't know. However, I began to get the message that it was time 'to move on.' It was a very lonely time." Grief takes as long as it takes. In order to grieve well, we must not try to block it; it must flow until it flows clean. Only then can there be space for the new life to come.

Much has been written about the "stages" of grief. Although there may be some merit in such models, grief swirls around in ways that are not neatly separated. One image for grief is that of an *estuary*. The Hudson River is, in fact, not a river—it is an estuary—an arm of the sea where salty sea water meets the fresh water running off the land. The rising and falling tides continually reverse, and the layers of fresh water and salt water are always shifting. This is like grief—it does not flow in one direction, and it comes in layers that are ever shifting.

The poet, May Sarton, describes the riches that loss can bring:

> Partaking wisdom, I have been given
> The sum of many difficult acts of grace,
> A vital fervor disciplined to patience.
> This cup holds grief and balm in equal measure.
> Light, darkness. Who drinks from it must change.
> Yet I am lavish in riches made from loss.[1]

Loss can bring both grief and balm. Light and darkness can exist together. When we look back on the longer view of our losses, we can begin to see more clearly the many acts of grace that have brought us to where we are.

The secure base of God's love will not take away our losses, but it can help us discover an abiding Presence that sustains us, even in the midst of things that are passing away. Our losses can give us hidden riches: a gratitude for every precious moment of life; a sense that all is a gift to be treasured; a deepened empathy for others without giving words of false comfort. These are not riches we have chosen; they, like our losses, have come unbidden, sometimes unexpectedly.

Ultimately, in this fleeting life all *is* lost. Our loves, our labors, our hopes and dreams, all are carried away. In learning, over and over, to let go of what we cannot keep from losing, our farewells are somehow gathered into the heart of Love where they are redeemed and made a gateway into life. "Weeping may linger for the night, but joy comes with the morning" (Psalm 30:5). In some way too mysterious for comprehension, even loss can become an entrance to a deeper, richer life. We cannot escape change and loss, but if we become more rooted and grounded in love, we have a secure base from which nothing can take us. Theresa of Avila encourages us with these words:

> Let nothing disturb you,
> Let nothing frighten you,
> All things are passing away:
> God never changes.
> Patience obtains all things.
> Whoever has God lacks nothing;
> God alone suffices.[2]

All things pass away; only love remains. In letting ourselves be loved by God, we build upon a solid rock that will support and sustain us whatever life and death may bring.

PRAYER

My God,
I can never prepare myself for loss;
It is always wrenching,
disorienting.
But help me to trust
that each loss can teach me
not to cling so tightly;
to let go, to fall
into the unknown
where you lie waiting
to meet me.
All will be lost:
my loved ones,
my body, my life.
But you have promised
that all that is lost
will be found again in you.
Help me find the riches
hidden in my loss,
the rock-certainty of your love
in the swirling rapids of change.
Help me to lose
that I may gain.
May all my losses
lead me back to you.

CHAPTER 6

FEAR OF LOVING OURSELVES

You shall love your neighbor as yourself.
—Matthew 19:19

Distortions in our religious traditions have promoted the mistaken idea that it is somehow bad—perhaps even dangerous—to love ourselves "too much." Popular misconceptions abound about God wanting us to think little of ourselves in order to be favored and approved. Don't the scriptures tell us that "those who humble themselves will be exalted" (Luke 14:11)? The problem is how we understand humility. Our English word *humility* is linked to the root word *humus* meaning earth, ground. It means being planted in the Ground of our Being, knowing ourselves to be rooted in our creaturehood, and needing first to receive love before we can give it. Unfortunately, certain misguided religious teachings have given us a shame-based idea of humility in which we should dampen our healthy sense of self. Humility becomes linked with a sense of shame, while a healthy love of self is confused with self-absorption and self-centeredness. Yet, the opposite is the case: the more we are able to love and respect ourselves as a gift from God, the more we are able to love others. This was wonderfully demonstrated by Sarah, the three-and-a-half-year-old daughter of friends, who unabashedly declared her love for herself during her bedtime prayers. As she and her mother were saying their evening prayers, she stretched out her arms as wide as she could and said, "I love Daddy *this* much!" Then, "I love Mommy *this* much!" And then—"I love myself *this* much!" Her mother filled with tears to see her daughter loving herself so freely—in a way she had not been able to as a child. She saw in the fresh exuberance of her daughter the precious gift that so many of us lose so early: the passionate love of ourselves rooted in the goodness of creation.

Self-hatred is a serious and destructive spiritual malady. Because it so often masquerades as goodness—as humility, love of others, avoidance of attention, and so on— it is often difficult to recognize self-hatred and its harmful effects. We tolerate its insidious presence, mistaking it as a virtue, while it undermines our healthy love of self. As a psychotherapist, I sometimes point out to clients the great price they pay for their self-hurting attitudes and behaviors. For example:

- A woman wins an award but immediately disparages her own accomplishments.
- A man refuses to develop his own talents, wallowing in passivity and resentment.
- A woman prides herself on forgiving others, yet refuses to forgive herself for falling short of her own expectations.

We often do not recognize these actions as self-hating, because they are so ingrained and unconscious. However, as we become more aware of the ways in which we undermine and hurt ourselves, we can develop greater compassion toward ourselves. Sometimes, it is important to remind my clients that they would be outraged if they saw someone hurting another person in the way they hurt themselves!

Ultimately, our attack upon ourselves is an attack upon God, a refusal to accept the self that God has made. There is a Hasidic saying that a host of angels goes in a vanguard before every human being crying out, "Make way! Make way for the image of God!" When we attack ourselves, we are attacking the image of God within us, an image we are called to treasure and nourish in ourselves and others.

The Scottish psychoanalyst W. R. D. Fairbairn, believes that our self-hatred can sometimes be a way of "keeping mother or father good." As children, we are radically dependent on our parents and so need to see them as good and dependable. The thought of being dependent on a parent who is unpredictable, unloving, perhaps even abusive, is so frightening that the child instead idealizes the parent—keeps mother or father "good"—while taking the parents' badness into the self, where the child tries to control this badness by making it his or her own. The child's reasoning says: It is better for me to be bad than for my parents and, by extension, the whole world to be bad. As Fairbairn puts it:

> It is better to be a sinner in a world ruled by a good God, than to live in a world ruled by the Devil. A sinner in a world ruled by God may be bad; but there is always a certain sense of security to be derived from the fact that the world around is good....In a world ruled by the Devil...[we] can have no sense of security and no hope of redemption.[1]

Self-hatred can also be fueled by an unrealistic perfectionism. A young woman described it this way: "I feel as though I'm either on a pedestal or in the pit. I believe no one will love me unless I am perfect, but when I fail, I feel utterly worthless." As she explored the hurtful consequences of these irrational extremes, she came to see that her "pedestal" and her "pit" were actually both manifestations of her underlying desire to control reality and shape it to her will. Only as she began to relinquish her idol of absolute control could she begin to accept herself and others as a mixture of weakness and strength. Only by abandoning both her pedestal and her pit could she simply "join the human race," and know that she had infinite worth simply because she existed, not because of her own impossible standards.

Our self-hatred is a refusal to accept our preciousness in God's sight, substituting our own self-absorbed judgment for God's mercy. We turn a withering judgment upon ourselves, refusing to have what Francis de Sales calls "meekness toward ourselves":

> Many people...when overcome by anger... become angry at being angry, disturbed at being disturbed, and vexed at being vexed. By such means they keep their hearts drenched and steeped in passion. It may seem that the second fit of anger does away with the first, but actually it serves to open the way for fresh anger on the first occasion that arises....We must be sorry for our faults in a calm, settled, firm way.[2]

Repenting of our self-hatred involves dethroning ourselves from the ultimate judgment seat, extending to ourselves the same mercy we would extend to others.

Feelings of self-hatred may masquerade as false humility. We can project our self-thwarting attitudes onto God, thinking God expects us to put ourselves down. Any stirrings of self-love are squashed, because we think they take us away from God's will. God then becomes an ogre who delights in thwarting our natural desires and we become self-loathing doormats. However, when we let ourselves be loved, we discover that we are accepted as we are. Paul Tillich speaks of how we often become aware of God's liberating acceptance when we are feeling most trapped in our self-hatred and self-frustration:

> Sometimes at that moment a wave of light breaks into our darkness, and it is as though a voice were saying, "You are accepted. You are accepted by that which is greater than you, and the name of which you do not know. Do not ask for the name now; perhaps you will find it later. Do not try to do anything now; perhaps later you will do much. Do not seek for anything; do not perform anything; do not intend anything. Simply accept the fact that you are accepted. If that happens to us, we experience grace.[3]

Grace breaks in when we least anticipate it. God's love is stunning and disorienting as it streams into our darkness, accepting us as we are. As we open to love, we find something surprising: instead of ironing out the wrinkles of our character—our neurotic wounds, our anxieties, and our peculiar psychic "dead ends"—love enlivens us *as we are*. We are breathed into by the Spirit of Life, set upon our feet to stand before God and the world in all the glory and vulnerability of our true selves. We had imagined that we would become some other sort of person—that we could escape the bedeviling flaws of our character. Instead, we discover that those "flaws" are the very openings through which love can touch us to the core of our being.

PRAYER

Forgive me, my God,
for not loving myself
as I ought.
I have failed to treasure myself,
to have compassion on myself.
I have failed to recognize
my acts of self-hatred,
rationalizing them as necessary,
even good and holy.
Teach me to love myself,
to respect my infinite
preciousness,
for in loving myself
I honor you.
In venerating your sacred presence
within me,
I venerate your presence
in all things.

CHAPTER 7

FEAR OF JOY

If you suddenly and unexpectedly feel joy, don't hesitate. Give in to it...don't be afraid of its plenty. Joy is not made to be a crumb.[1]

—Mary Oliver

Why would anyone fear joy? It seems absurd. Don't we all desire joy? As strange as it seems, I have found in myself and others both a desire and a fear of joy. This fear of joy can be another obstacle to letting ourselves be loved. We frequently express our fear of joy in phrases like, "Things are going too well; I'm waiting for the other shoe to drop; If I'm too happy, I'll tempt the Fates; If I'm too successful, I'm afraid I will have to pay for it; I feel guilty for enjoying my life when others are suffering so much." These phrases express a fear that joy is risky, because it may be cut off at any time. It is better to live with the volume turned down and one's expectations lowered than to experience joy to the full, only to have it snatched away.

Fear of joy sometimes signals the presence of what family therapist Ivan Boszormenyi-Nagy, calls "invisible loyalties."[2] Our loyalty to family members—especially to those who are unhappy and wounded—makes us feel as though we are abandoning them in their misery if we move on and have a full and joyful life.

49

I once heard a rabbi speak of a man in his congregation who came to unburden himself of the guilt he felt over surviving his brother. As young men, he and his older brother had been interred together in a Nazi concentration camp. His brother had devised a plan of escape in which they would scale the large wall surrounding the prison. On the day of their planned escape, the younger brother watched in horror as his brother went ahead of him and climbed onto the wall only to be instantly electrocuted. Years later, the younger brother had been freed by the Allied Forces and had moved to America, but he still felt as though he had no right to live his life, since his brother's life had been cut short so tragically. The rabbi assured him that he was in no way guilty of his brother's death and that his brother would not begrudge him his happiness. However, the man's guilt persisted. Several months after visiting the rabbi, he had a heart attack and required heart surgery. His doctors gave him a hopeful prognosis, but were puzzled when he seemed to be slipping into a postoperative coma. By all medical reasoning, he should be recovering, yet each day he seemed to be moving closer and closer to death. During one of his hospital visits, the rabbi asked to spend some time alone with the man. He held his hand and told him that it was time to let go of his brother, that his brother did not begrudge him his life, and that it was time to stop carrying his dead brother on his back. He told the man that his family needed him; it was time to let the dead go and return to the land of the living. The next day, the man rallied and soon returned to a fully active life.

Our invisible loyalties bind us not only to the dead, but also to the living. If my parents are unhappy or self-thwarting, who am I to leave them behind after all they have done for me? How can I abandon them to their suffering and move on with my own life? It is a painful thing to surrender our loved ones to God's care, knowing that we are not called to sacrifice our own growth in order to make them whole. If we make such a misguided self-sacrifice, we unconsciously perpetuate our family legacy of self-enfeeblement and unlived life. Sometimes, parents themselves send out guilty mixed messages that say, "I am so proud of you, but here I am left behind while you do what I never could." Unconscious or "invisible" loyalties make us keep our foot on the brake, afraid to surpass our wounded parents. To the degree that we transfer our experience with our parents onto God, we fear that God will also begrudge us our joy and will drop the "next shoe" on us just when we are feeling most joyful and alive.

When my friend Benedict suggested that I replace my prerecorded image of God with an image of God delighting to be with me, something in me recoiled, thinking this was "too good to be true." As I sat in the stillness, I kept expecting the "other shoe to drop." Something bad was bound to happen if I sat alone with God. If I felt too good, God would begrudge me my joy. Such a view of God has more in common with the Greek gods, who felt threatened by mortals' successes, than the God proclaimed in the words of the early Christian theologian Irenaeus: "The glory of God is the human person fully alive."[3]

Besides our fear of surpassing those we love, we may fear joy simply because it is new, spacious, and unfamiliar. Like a caged animal that has grown used to its confined world and does not venture far once set free, we become accustomed to living small, predictable lives without zest and delight. However, this is not the vision of life held out in John's Gospel, where Jesus prays that we "may have life, and have it abundantly" (John 10:10), and that his joy may be made complete in us (John 17:13). Letting ourselves be loved means opening ourselves to the fullness of life with all its joys and sorrows, beauty, hilarity, tenderness, heights, and depths.

The fear of joy is—like most of our fears—stubborn and irrational. We cannot get rid of it simply by telling ourselves it makes no sense. The old inner voices of fear and hidden loyalty continue to echo within us. When beset by these joy-denying voices within us, we need to listen to the voice of Love that is stronger than our shame and fear, reminding us that, no matter what next "shoe" of circumstance may drop, God never begrudges us our joy.

PRAYER

My God,
I have feared joy.
I have held back from
the fullness of life,
bound by invisible threads
of old loyalties.
I have imagined that you
begrudge me my joy and fulfillment,
that you would intentionally
disrupt my happiness,
stifle my freedom
and rein in my delight.
Now I see that you
have always been calling me forth
like Lazarus from the tomb:
"Untie him and let him go!"
You desire the fullness of
life for me,

abundant, overflowing.
Unbind me, free me for joy,
that I may be fully alive.
You have held nothing back from me.
Help me to hold nothing
back in this life,
to live it to the fullest,
to drink deeply of joy—
your joy which you desire
to share with me forever.

CHAPTER 8

FEAR OF DOUBT AND DARKNESS

Doubt is not the opposite of faith; it is one element of faith.

—Paul Tillich

There are times when life presents us with new questions that our old answers cannot satisfy. Our prayers are not answered as we hope: we are confronted with things we cannot understand. This happens particularly as we confront suffering and tragedy both on a personal level and in the world around us. In the face of sickness, innocent suffering, natural disasters, accidents, and the death of the innocent, we may ask, "Why do bad things happen to good people?" It is a question posed by Job. When he experiences manifold calamities, his friends try to convince him that there is some reason for his suffering, that it is "God's will," but Job resists this easy explanation, knowing he cannot reconcile his awful fate with his abiding belief in the goodness of God.

A young woman in her early twenties was married in a large, joyous wedding. The church was packed; there was exhilaration in the air. The bride and groom were flowering in their early adult lives together, launched in successful careers with a bright future before them. Then just a month later, the young bride suddenly developed a mysterious lung infection and died within a few days. It seemed unreal and unbelievable. The same crowd that had celebrated her wedding a few weeks before now gathered in the same packed church for her funeral. Such tragedies make us cry out, "Where are you God in all of this? Don't you care? Are you there at all?"

Doubt can also be cognitive. New learning may expose us to new ideas, and new experiences may force us to question old assumptions. When we are faced with new information, we have a choice to either block it out or begin integrating it into our worldview. Regardless of our questions and uncertainties and their origins, Thomas "the Doubter" can be a helpful model of faithful doubt. We sometimes speak of a "Doubting Thomas" as someone who is overly negative and skeptical; however the gospel description does not bear this out. Instead, Thomas is a person who will not take important things simply on other people's reports. If he is to believe, he must have an experience of his own that is personally convincing. Thomas is absent when the risen Christ shows himself to his disciples. Excitedly they tell him, "We have seen the Lord!" However, it is a "we" that does not include a "me." Thomas dares to doubt—he needs to know for himself. He asks to put his fingers in the nail marks in Jesus' body and Jesus, far from berating him, makes himself available to be touched and seen.

Times of disequilibrium confront us with a world beyond our control and comprehension. Like Alice in Wonderland falling down the rabbit hole, the familiar and dependable collapse under us and we lose our balance and fall, not knowing where we will land. At first, Alice is afraid that she will never land; then she is afraid that she will land and be destroyed on impact. I remember a time of doubt in my own life when I felt as if I were falling down a rabbit hole. My trust in life was shaken; I was profoundly disillusioned. How could God allow this to happen? What had seemed like solid ground was suddenly collapsing underneath me like a trap door. I felt as if I were free-falling down a dark tunnel, plummeting into the unknown. As I fell, I sent out a desperate prayer: "God, if you are there, let me know and feel your presence. I can no longer make myself believe. I am letting go, but I am not sure if you will be there to catch me." As I fell through inner space, I felt the terror of letting go of all my preconceived ideas about how things should be; I let go of everything I had been trying to sustain through my own power. After a dizzying time of free fall, I suddenly felt a jolt: I was being caught and held by Loving Hands. There was Someone there besides me! Someone bigger than my doubts and fears was now meeting me exactly at the point of my helplessness and need. I knew that this was not my own doing. I had hit rock bottom—and it was Love.

Of course, this was not my last fall down the rabbit hole! Periodically the ground rumbles beneath my feet and I realize that my world is once again opening up. It is time again to fall further into the mystery of life. However, with each new fall, I carry with me the memory of God's sustaining presence. Although I may feel frightened and disoriented, a voice within tells me that this loss, too, can be another fall into grace.

It is a mistake to think that feeling doubt means that we do not have enough faith. Instead, these difficult times can be the necessary portal through which we can pass into a deeper relationship with God. As contradictory as it may seem, our doubt can be the fruit of our faith and prayer, because God desires to lead us to a more radical trust and love. This is why John of the Cross sees the Dark Night of the Soul not as a darkness of our own creating but as God's response to our desire to grow closer. In this night, God strips us of our old ways of understanding and the consolations of God's presence we once felt. For John, this painful disorientation is a necessary death that calls us to deepened dependency on God.[1]

When we experience the breakdown of our way of making sense of things, we can feel despair. We can see no way through. This was what Karl Rahner experienced during World War II as he saw civilization crumbling around him, descending into a maelstrom of evil as Nazism swept through his native Germany. He huddled with others in crowded, dark cellars as the air strikes blazed across the skies. In this time of great social upheaval, Rahner also felt an upheaval in his soul and experienced God's painful silence. As he faced the limits of his comprehension and the apparent silence of God, Rahner realized he must not run from his despair if his faith was to be genuine. He must face it and go into it. He gives this counsel:

> For look, if you stand firm, if you don't run away from despair—then you will become aware that you're not buried alive at all—that this deathly emptiness is only a disguise for an intimacy of God's, that God's silence...is filled by the Word without words, by [God] who is above all names, by [God] who is all in all. And God's silence is telling you that God is here.[2]

Times of doubt are invitations to imagine a bigger God, a God more mysterious than our small minds can contain. As Moses fell on his face at the burning bush, he asked for God's name, but was given only this answer: "I am who

I am." The Hebrews stressed that God's name could not be uttered because language could not fully contain God.

Rahner suggests that even our word *God* can get used too freely, as if we think we fully know God. *God* becomes a household word, which we throw around lightly. Instead, Rahner suggests that the term *Holy Mystery* can remind us that God is a mystery beyond our comprehension. Mystery does not mean that we know nothing, but rather that we always know in part. "For now we see in a mirror, dimly, but then we will see face to face. Now I know only in part; then I will know fully, even as I have been fully known" (1 Corinthians 13:12). St. Paul concludes his passage by saying that even though we know partially, the greatest abiding power is love: "Now faith, hope, and love abide, these three; and the greatest of these is love." In letting ourselves be loved, we allow ourselves to be embraced by Holy Mystery, drawn into God's love that is beyond our comprehension, yet closer to us than breathing. The anonymous author of *The Cloud of Unknowing* says that there is a limit to what our intellect can grasp of God, because there is always a "cloud of unknowing" that stands between us and God. The only way to penetrate this cloud is through *love*.

> God may be reached and held close by means of love, but by means of thought never.

Although this cloud may block us from full understanding of God, this does not mean that we are separated from God. The writer exhorts us to "storm heaven" with our longing for God:

> Strike the thick Cloud of Unknowing with a sharp dart of longing love and do not retreat no matter what comes to pass.[3]

In this life it is only through love, not full knowledge, that we may experience God. Spiritual doubt and darkness, however painful, are invitations to allow ourselves to be loved and led in ways we cannot comprehend. Sometimes the way is dark, but John of the Cross believes that the night is a "radiant darkness." His words echo those of the psalmist: "Even the darkness is not dark to you; the night is as bright as the day, for darkness is as light to you" (Psalm 139:12). Although we may feel lost and do not know where we are going, somehow we are being led by God in a way we cannot presently see. Thomas Merton describes this in a prayer:

> My God I have no idea where I am going. I do not see the road ahead of me. I cannot know for certain where it will end...but I believe that...you will lead me by the right road, though I may know nothing of it.[4]

Because we are the Beloved, our doubt and darkness will never separate us from the love of God. Things may come and go, and the unknown and unfamiliar may unsettle us. Questions may remain unanswered. We may feel alone, doubting, and unsure, but doubt and darkness are not the last word. God's love will never let us go, even when we are uncertain and lost.

PRAYER

O God, new questions have arisen in my life
which the old answers cannot satisfy.
What used to feel like firm ground
has fallen away under my feet.

Life has brought me experiences
that I cannot make sense of;
I feel unsure and sometimes lost.
There is an empty space where I once was full;
doubt where I once believed.
Where are you in all this?
Are you even here at all?
Help me to wait in this darkness,
not to run from it,
to be honest, to be courageous
and not shrink from this uncertain time.
I need a new experience of your love and presence.
Let your love find me in this darkness,
lead me on this unfamiliar path
even when I cannot see you doing so.
Although I may feel lost,
help me wait for you to reveal your love;
for you are my way, my truth, my life.

CHAPTER 9

FEAR OF AGING AND DEATH

We must overcome death by finding God in it….Teach
me to treat my death as an act of communion.
—Pierre Teilhard de Chardin

If we live long enough, diminishment will come to us all. Time takes its toll: parts wear out and senses grow dimmer. We are aware that the clock is ticking. Where we used to take time for granted, we realize there is less and less of it. As we diminish, we learn more and more that we are in the grip of what we used to be able to grasp. We often live with a certain denial of our death, which may be necessary if we are to live fully in the present. When Carl Jung was asked what advice he would give to the aging, he responded, "Live on as if you were going to live forever. Look forward to tomorrow…we cannot stand a meaningless life."[1] However, Jung also believed that the later part of life requires a different focus from the one we had in our youth:

> We cannot live the afternoon of our lives according to the programme of life's morning. The afternoon of life must also have a significance of its own and cannot be merely a pitiful appendage to life's morning.[2]

The significance of the morning of our lives is our development as an individual in establishing ourselves in the world, but the afternoon and the evening require us to adjust our attitude and find meaning in a new way. Our time is limited: What are we going to do with the rest of it? What matters most? When my parents died—each at the same age—I "checked the odometer" and realized I had more mileage on me than I had thought! I had never done the math before. It was shocking. Given genetics, I might live a little longer than my parents, perhaps less, but now I could count my life in just a few decades, not the seemingly endless future that lies before us in our youth.

Aging brings us face to face with the inevitability of diminishment. Paradoxically, this diminishment may also be a time of new fruitfulness and wisdom. We can begin to winnow through our experience and see what is of lasting value and what we can let go of. Our heightened sense of the preciousness of life can help us marshal our energies, think about what really matters at this time, what we still hope to accomplish, and what expectations we may need to adjust. As we age, there are choices to make about our attitude. Will we become a boring or enjoyable older person to be with? Will we become complainers with our tedious and repetitive reports of our ailments, our laments about the present state of the world, and our nostalgia for "the good old days"? Or will we become more like the elders who we find interesting and energizing? They are less self-absorbed, take themselves more lightly, and often have a sense of playful irony. They have lived much and have much to share, but are also open to learning more. I saw this in my mother's indomitable spirit. She was always a planner and a doer, always curious about the world. She was an avid genealogist and, although by eighty her health was beginning to fail, she was determined that we make a final pilgrimage back to our ancestral Scotland. She was fully alive when she died.

Aging is no excuse for withdrawing from life or playing it safe. It can be an opportunity for greater authenticity. We can find greater freedom in being ourselves, caring less about what people think of us and speaking our mind honestly. Our later years can be a time of great generativity. Whatever has grown riper in us over time is to be shared with the world. We can be like seedpods in autumn—although they are dry and seem spent, they can burst open with new life that they scatter all around them. We can choose to keep giving and receiving life, and remaining curious about the world around us. In her book *Let Evening Come*, Mary Morrison writes this reflection at the age of 85:

> With nothing to gain or lose...we find that we have new eyes if we only lose old habits, take up new ones, and become curiouser and curiouser. We have been granted, before we leave this world, a chance to look—really look—at it, and see it freshly...tasting all the miracles that have always been.[3]

However, all this does not override the painful and annoying deterioration of our bodies. Morrison gives a colorful description of getting out of bed in the morning:

> Ok, so I got out of bed today. I opened one eye—my half-blind eye, for some reason. I checked myself out here and there...I stood up, but fell back on the bed—it always takes two tries—stood up again...at eighty-five it takes a while to regain the upright posture which we learned at age one.[4]

Aging calls us to a deeper humility. We must take our place in the cycle of life for time will make no exception for us. We come and go from this earth, but life continues. Growing old is an opportunity to learn to trust more deeply that life is not something that we create; it is something that lives *through us*.

As we age, it is critical to base our lives on being loved and esteemed by God, not on others' opinions of us, or even our opinion of ourselves. As we become "those" people we viewed as the "elderly," it is essential to realize that our worth does not lie in our productivity, our looks, or our "usefulness." We are the Beloved—that is our true, unshakeable identity, no matter how we or others see us. We must let ourselves be loved as we are, for with time slipping away, it becomes increasingly evident that we can be no one but ourselves.

Pierre Teilhard de Chardin speaks of God "hallowing our diminishments." God works not only through what we *can* do but also what we *cannot* do. He likens this hallowing to "an artist who makes use of a fault or an impurity [while] sculpting...so as to produce more exquisite lines or a more beautiful tone."[5] We must surrender again and again to the carver's invisible hand that seeks to bring out the deep grain of love in us. We ourselves are the work of art we are creating with God. All our cracks, wounds, and imperfections can be used by God to bring out more beauty in us.

Teilhard said, "We must overcome death by finding God in it....Teach me to treat my death as an act of communion."[6] This is what my friend Alex did as he fought stomach cancer. He persevered valiantly, undergoing treatment after treatment, until there was no more hope of recovery. As he made this painful journey, something remarkable happened. He started a blog and began to share his experiences with an ever-widening group of people. He shared not only his medical developments, but also his spiritual journey in wrestling with disease and dying. His entries had a candor and freshness that never felt self-indulgent or self-pitying. He helped those of us who read his frequent updates to embrace and share with each other the full gambit of our humanity: with its delight and sorrow, humor and depression, celebration and agony. He shared with us the pearl of great price born of his suffering, speaking often about what he called "the Big Love." Although Alex finally could not eat, his dying became a banquet of love, a Eucharist of redemption in the midst of suffering: "This is my body which is given for you; do this for the remembrance of me." This is what Alex had given us in his dying. It was a communion shared by us all.

Whatever the mystery that awaits us when we die, one thing is for sure: death does not end a relationship. "Love is strong as death....Many waters cannot quench love, neither can floods drown it" (Song of Songs 8:6–7). Love cannot drown out our love for those we have lost. Mysteriously, there is still some active relationship of mutual love and concern, which transcends the limits of time and space. This is sometimes called "the Communion of Saints." When my father died, I performed the ancient ritual of the Anointing of the Senses on his body as the brilliant morning sun streamed into the church. I marked "the seats of the senses"—his eyes, his mouth, his ears, his hands, and his feet. This is a traditional symbol of being cleansed from all one's sins committed through any of these senses. It is a tender act, and as I performed it, I thought of all the miles my father's feet had walked, all the sights his eyes had seen, all the words he had said, all the sounds he had heard, and all he had touched with his hands. I thought of his hands holding me as a child, and now our roles were reversed: I was putting him to rest, as he had often put me to bed and prayed for my safety during the night. I prayed for him, wept over him, and gave thanks for him. I had a similar experience with my mother, as we gathered around in her final hours. Although she was unconscious—at least in some ways, for we know that people in a deep coma can often hear and remember—we sang to her, stroked her hair, soothed her the way one would when putting a baby to sleep. Dying holds a striking similarity to birthing: everyone waits upon the breath—to begin or end. The end and the beginning are joined in a sacred circle. Such is the mystery of the unbreakable bond of the Communion of Saints.

Many people have described experiences of what the Celts call "thin places," where the veil between this world and some greater, more amazing world is lifted—often only for a fleeting, tantalizing moment. When we try to imagine a greater life beyond this one, we can only speak in terms of unknowing and paradox: "No eye has seen, nor ear heard, nor the human heart conceived, what God has prepared for those who love him" (1 Corinthians 2:9). It is a Mystery we cannot fathom. For now, all we can do is stand in awe, longing for the portals where we hope to glimpse into the Heart of things; when some veil will be lifted and we will behold the power and the glory that is always there, but which now we cannot fully see.

At the end of his *Confessions*, Augustine of Hippo paints a beautiful picture of the Endless Sabbath in which the sun will never set:

> Give us peace, Lord God, for you have given us all else; give us the peace that is repose, the peace of the Sabbath, and the peace that knows no evening….And then you will rest in us, as now

you work in us....For you Lord are ever working, ever resting.[7]

Augustine pictures God not only working in us but *resting* in us—what a beautiful image! God desires to be in us, rest in us, make a home in us, to give us new life on the unending eighth day of Creation. This is not a rest that is the end of life, for Creation is never over. We are part of that ongoing creation. The rest of the Endless Sabbath is not a passive rest; it is a rest that is always working—transforming us more and more into the image of Divine Love.

Death is our final act of letting ourselves be loved. It is an invitation to trust God more and more deeply, to *believe* that "all will be well and all manner of things will be well."[8] Death is our greatest act of dependence on God in which we must let ourselves be loved in all our vulnerability. It is our ultimate surrender, in which we must relinquish all control. We can do nothing but let ourselves be loved, trusting only in God's grace and love.

Prayer

O God of all my years,
My aging brings me new pains,
New loss of power.
As my years grow fewer,
Give me gratitude for each new day.
May I treasure the time,
Choose wisely,
Speak honestly,
Dare greatly,
That I may be fully alive when I die.

Help me bend flexibly in the winds of time.
To share the fruits of my living—
The ripe seeds of life
That have grown in me through many years.
Save me from self-pity,
Bitterness, and regret.
Hallow my diminishment.
With your carver's hand,
Bring out the deep grain of love in me.

When evening comes
May my death be an act of communion.
As I approach my end,
Hold my trembling heart in your hands.
When I am afraid
Let me hear you speaking in my heart:
"You are my Beloved!"
May my fall into death
Be a fall into the abyss of your bottomless love.
Hold me, lead me, envelop me, and penetrate me,
Take me to your self.
O my Beginning and my End,
O Life of my Life,
O Love that will not let me go,
Hold me now and at the hour of my death.
Hold me tightly to yourself.
And bid me come to you.

EPILOGUE

The Great Round Dance of Love

Love is a conversion to humanity...the choice to experience life as a member of the human family, a partner in the dance of life.

—Carter Heyward

In the noncanonical scripture, "The Acts of John,"[1] Jesus dances with his disciples the night before his arrest. He stands in the middle while they join hands and circle around him. He tells them, "Whoever does not dance does not know what is coming to pass." Like a wheel spinning around its hub, they dance around and around while he sings to them of his coming death and resurrection. They form a living mandala: hand in hand, in the great Round Dance of Love, with the dying and rising Christ at the center, singing to them of inevitable loss and gain.

When trying to describe the dynamic life of the Trinity, some early theologians employed the Greek word *perichoresis*, meaning "to dance around." The Trinity is that loving energy at the heart of reality that forms an endless circle of dance; each person distinct and yet all forming a greater whole. Picture the huge, exuberant Matisse cutouts of dancers whirling hand in hand, and you have an image of the Trinity!

Dance is a wonderful symbol for connection and separateness. When we dance, we touch; we synchronize movements, and yet we also allow space for each other. Too much space between us and our dance becomes isolated solos; too little space between us and we crowd each other. Dancing can be awkward; we can hurt each other, pulling and pushing. In our daily dance of intimacy with spouses, family, community, and friends, we sometimes step on each other and we get stepped on. However, there are also the graced moments when we feel ourselves moving together: the dinner where everyone is laughing, relaxed, glad to be together; the roughhousing or snuggling with lovers, children, pets; precious, unexpected moments when we feel ourselves in tune with Creation, dancing with life; neither pushing nor pulling. At these moments we embody the great Dance of Love, where there is room for all. We move with a shared grace. This Dance includes our whole human family, with its rich diversity of race, creed, class, and sexuality.

The image of dancing in a circle expresses a mysterious truth about love: the more we give love, the more we receive it, and the more we receive love, the more we give it. At times, we have to rouse ourselves to love others, moving beyond our own negativity and self-preoccupation; to push ourselves "beyond ourselves" in order to love. At other times, we are not able to "get beyond ourselves"; we are overwhelmed by crisis, illness, stress, and grief. At these times, we need someone to reach out to us, and to do for us what we cannot do for ourselves. Throughout our lives, we never stop needing both to receive and to give love. If we imagine that we are more in need of either giving or receiving love, we still have not understood the divine economy of love. It is a seamless circle in which all givers are receivers, and all receivers are givers. In the Dance of Love there is radical equality: all are both active and receptive, both subject and object, both lover and Beloved.

Each day brings a new invitation to dance with Love. As we face the unknown hours that lie before us, the demons of anxiety and expectation assault us. They trouble us with projected scenarios of imagined problems: What will I do if *this* happens? What will I do if this *does not* happen? There is no way to anticipate the challenges of each day. Our worst fears will rarely prove to be accurate. Our most delicious fantasies will rarely come to pass. Things may be much better and much worse than we imagine. All the changes and chances of life are transitory. Only love remains.

The daily Dance of Love cannot be learned ahead of time; the steps must be taken one at a time. We are tempted to skip over a step in order to get to the part where we think we will be more secure. However, the Dance cannot be rushed, nor can it be slowed down. It has its own pace. As we dance, we find ourselves surprised by love. An unexpected person, event, or insight transforms the whole day and we see the world with new eyes.

In letting ourselves be loved, we take the hand of every other creature and circle around the Mysterious Center. It is a great paradox of human growth that the more we discover ourselves, the more open we become to life. The journey "inward" leads us to that point of intersection where we realize our vital connection with life. We are continually being summoned to play our part, to embrace our life's work more completely and, in the process, touch others' lives more deeply. The vocation to fulfill our own potential and the call to love others is one and the same. Learning to join hands with all of creation in the Divine Dance is exactly why we are here. It is only in this Dance that we find life's deepest meaning. In the swirling choreography that links quarks to galaxies, we each have our part to play in this amazing performance. In letting ourselves be loved, we return to our true Center, surrendering our fears again and again, discovering a new strength rising up within us even as our old false confidence falls away. At the very point of failing at our own self-invented fantasies of success, power, and control, we find a small opening into the Greater Life—the narrow entrance through which we pass into the vast spaciousness of Love.

APPENDIX

A Meditation on
Letting Yourself Be Loved

Sit quietly in a comfortable position. Let yourself relax, gently allowing yourself to enter the silence. Begin to recite the following phrases, letting their meaning sink in slowly:

> God, I am your Beloved,
> made in your image.
> You delight in being with me
> as I am.
> Enfold me in your presence;
> shower me with your tenderness
> and unconditional love.

Allow the truth of these words to touch you. Open your heart and let God love you. If distractions, worries, or other thoughts come, simply let them be, returning your awareness to God's love for you in the moment. If you find it difficult to focus these thoughts on yourself, imagine that you are someone else looking at you. Pray these words for yourself as you would for someone else you love.

Pray this prayer regularly, letting the awareness of God's love permeate you. Do not worry about feeling or experiencing anything in particular. Whatever happens or doesn't happen is your own prayer. In time, try extending the prayer toward others, beginning with those close to you. Bring to mind someone you love and pray the prayer for him or her:

> *N.* is God's Beloved,
> made in God's image.
> God delights in being with *N.*
> as she or he is.
> Enfold *N.* in your presence;
> shower *N.* with your tenderness
> and unconditional love.

In time, try praying this prayer for others beyond your immediate circle, until you can extend it to people you find hard to love. Continue to pray this prayer regularly for yourself and others. You can pray it anytime, anywhere: in the car, at work, in a crowd, or while looking at a stranger. As you embrace the reality of being loved unconditionally, notice how your perception of others changes. The eyes of Love that gaze at you are the same eyes with which you will gaze upon others.[1]

NOTES

Introduction

1. D. W. Winnicott, "The Capacity To Be Alone," in *The Maturational Processes and the Facilitating Environment* (New York: International Universities Press, 1965), 29–36.

2. Johannes B. Metz, *Poverty of Spirit* (Mahwah, NJ: Paulist Press, 1968).

Chapter 1

1. T. S. Eliot, *Four Quartets* (New York: Harcourt, Brace & World, 1943), 57.

2. Frederick Buechner, "Adolescence and the Stewardship of Pain," in *The Clown in the Belfry* (San Francisco: Harper Collins, 1992), 83–104.

3. Henri Nouwen, *The Wounded Healer* (Garden City, NY: Image Books, 1979).

Chapter 2

1. Heinz Kohut, *The Restoration of the Self* (New York: International Universities Press, 1977).

2. Gerald May, *Addiction and Grace* (San Francisco: Harper and Row, 1988), 3ff. May provides an excellent discussion of attachment and self-image.

3. C. S. Lewis, *The Voyage of the Dawn Treader* (New York: Harper Trophy, 1994), 82–98.

Chapter 3

1. Pema Chodron, *The Wisdom of No Escape* (Boston: Shambala Publications, 1991).

2. Murray Bowen, *Family Therapy in Clinical Practice* (New York: Jason Aronson, 1978).

3. Martin Buber, *I and Thou* (New York: Charles Scribner's Sons, 1970).

4. John Bowlby, *A Secure Base* (New York: Basic Books, 1988). See also his *Attachment and Loss*, vols. 1–3 (New York: Basic Books, 1980).

Chapter 4

1. Madeleine L'Engle, *The Irrational Season* (New York: HarperOne, 1984), 55.

Chapter 5

1. May Sarton, *Collected Poems 1930–1973* (New York: WW Norton, 1974), 39.

2. Bookmark of Saint Teresa of Avila (1515–82).

Chapter 6

1. W. R. D. Fairbairn, *Psychoanalytic Studies of the Personality* (London & New York: Tavistock/Routledge, 1952/1990), 66–67.

2. Francis de Sales, *Introduction to the Devout Life* (New York: Image Books, 1989), 149–50.

3. Paul Tillich, "You are Accepted," in *The Shaking of the Foundations* (New York: Charles Scribner's Sons, 1948), 153–63.

Chapter 7

1. Mary Oliver, "Don't Hesitate," in *Swan: Poem and Prose Poems* (Boston: Beacon Press, 2010).

2. Ivan Boszormenyi-Nagy and Geraldine Spark, *Invisible Loyalties* (New York: Brunner/Mazel, 1984).

3. Irenaeus of Lyon, *Adversus Haereses*, IV, 34.

Chapter 8

1. *The Dark Night*, in *The Collected Works of St. John of the Cross* (Washington, DC: ICS Press, 1991).

2. Karl Rahner, *The Blessing and the Need of Prayer* (Collegeville, MN: The Liturgical Press, 1997), 3–8.

3. Ira Progoff, trans, *The Cloud of Unknowing* (New York: Dell Publishing, 1957), 72–73.

4. Thomas Merton, *Thoughts in Solitude* (New York: Farrar, Strauss & Giroux, 1999), 79.

Chapter 9

1. Carl Jung, interview by John Freeman, *Face to Face*, BBC, October 22, 1959.

2. C. G. Jung, *Collected Works*, vol. 8, (Princeton: Princeton University Press, 1957), 399.

3. Mary C. Morrison, *Let Evening Come: Reflections on Aging* (New York: Doubleday, 1998), 43–52.

4. Ibid., 45–46.

5. Pierre Teilhard de Chardin, *The Divine Milieu* (New York: Harper & Row, 1965), 86.

6. Ibid., 89–90.

7. St. Augustine of Hippo, *The Confessions*, trans. Maria Boulding, OSB (New York: Vintage Books, 1977), 341.

8. Julian of Norwich, *Showings* (New York: Paulist Press, 1978), 225.

Epilogue

1. Edgar Hennecke, Wilhelm Schneemelcher, and R. McL. Wilson, eds., *New Testament Apocrypha*, vol. 2 (Philadelphia: Westminster, 1964), 227–32.

Appendix

1. For a variation of this prayer drawn from the Buddhist tradition of "meta" or "loving-kindness" meditation, see Jack Kornfield, *A Path with Heart* (New York: Bantam Books, 1993), 19–21.